The Longparish Branch Line

Peter A. Harding

T9 class 4-4-0 No. 30730 passing under the loading gantry at Longparish Station in the early 1950's.
Lens of Sutton

Published by Peter A. Harding
Mossgiel, Bagshot Road, Knaphill
Woking, Surrey GU21 2SG

ISBN 0 9509414 8 4

© Peter A. Harding 1992
*Printed by Binfield Printers Ltd.,
Binfield Road, Byfleet, Surrey KT14 7PN*

Contents

	Page No.		Page No.
Introduction	3	The Branch in World War II	25
History of the Line	4	Final Closure	26
Description of the Route	11	The Present Scene	30
Motive Power & Rolling Stock	19	Conclusion	32
Operation	23	Acknowledgments	32
Timetables & Tickets	24	Bibliography	32

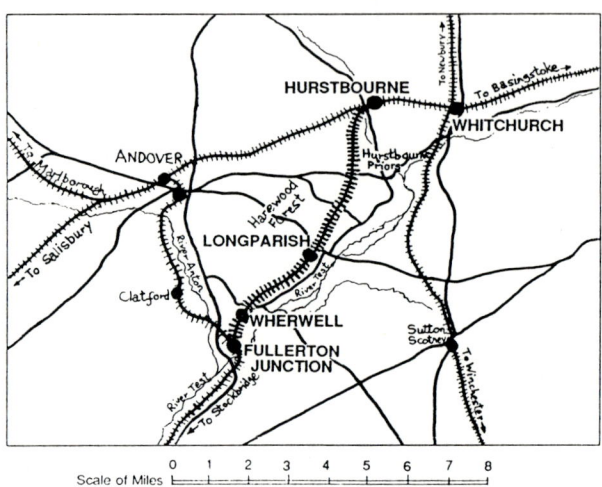

A special inspection train at Wherwell being propelled back from Longparish by T9 class 4-4-0 No. 30707 on October 30th 1957, seventeen months after the line was officially closed. S.C.Nash

Introduction

The attractive single track branch line which ran along the Test Valley in Hampshire from Fullerton to Longparish via Wherwell, was the remaining section of a double track through railway, which was opened by the London & South Western Railway in 1885, to connect their main West of England line, between Whitchurch and Andover at Hurstbourne, with their Andover to Redbridge line at Fullerton.

The original reason for building this through railway was to offer an alternative route to the one planned by the Didcot, Newbury & Southampton Railway who, having reached Newbury, wanted to continue their line south via Whitchurch to Southampton.

With plans for a connection between the two companies at Whitchurch, the London & South Western Railway felt that their Hurstbourne to Fullerton railway would not only give passengers a choice of reaching Southampton, but would also act as a defence should the Didcot, Newbury & Southampton Railway (backed by the Great Western Railway) cast their eyes towards Bournemouth and Weymouth.

As the connection between the two companies at Whitchurch was never built, the Hurstbourne to Fullerton line was doomed to failure before it really had chance to get started and, by way of economising, the line was singled in 1913 and the lightly used passenger service was withdrawn in 1931, although the goods service continued.

In 1934, the northern section between Hurstbourne and Longparish was taken out of use and lifted, making this once through railway into a rather basic country branch line, leaving the goods service between Fullerton and Longparish to continue until 1956.

A delightful view of some thatched roofed cottages at Wherwell, with the single track railway in the foreground. P. Trodd Collection

History of the Line

The whole history of railway development in this country is riddled with stories of two and sometimes even more separate railway companies bitterly opposing one another for the right to build their own line at the expense of their rivals. Quite often, the result was that many towns and villages were served by not only one but also a second company who had quite unnecessarily duplicated the route.

In the south of England, this particular practice was very evident in Kent during the latter part of the last century, when the South Eastern Railway and the London Chatham & Dover Railway played out their long standing feud by building many unnecessary, lightly used lines, purely as a defensive measure.

At about the same time, a slightly similar feud was taking place in Hampshire between the London & South Western Railway (LSWR) and the Great Western Railway (GWR). The LSWR were dominant in the county at the time, but were having great difficulty keeping the GWR at bay. With GWR eyes firmly set in the direction of Southampton, the LSWR would counter attack by preparing schemes to Bristol, where local businessmen were as fed up with the domination of the GWR as their counterparts in Southampton were with the LSWR.

Both companies put in various proposals but were unsuccessful until the GWR saw their chance to reach Southampton by way of the independent Didcot, Newbury & Southampton Junction Railway (DNSR). This company (who later dropped the word 'Junction' from their title) was authorised by an Act of August 5th 1873, to build a line from the GWR at Didcot, through Newbury and then south under the main LSWR Basingstoke - Salisbury line near Whitchurch and then join the main LSWR Basingstoke - Southampton line about $1^3/_4$ miles north of Micheldever Station. There was also plans for a junction with the LSWR Basingstoke - Salisbury line at Whitchurch.

The line opened from Didcot to Newbury on April 12th 1882, but the southern section was held up while various discussions took place with the Southampton Corporation, Harbour Board, Chamber of Commerce and other local businessmen who all wanted the DNSR to extend their independent line from Whitchurch to Southampton without depending on the LSWR, saying that an alternative railway linking Southampton with the Midlands and the North would be a profitable enterprise.

Taking these requests into consideration, the DNSR decided to seek powers to abandon the authorised southern section of the line to just north of Micheldever, and replace it with a direct line to Southampton via Winchester.

Spurred into action by this latest proposal from the DNSR, the LSWR came up with their own scheme to link Southampton with the Midlands and the North, which included a new line just over 7 miles long, to be built from the main LSWR Basingstoke - Salisbury line at Hurstbourne to a junction at Fullerton on the Andover & Redbridge Railway; a junction with the DNSR at Whitchurch (which was also part of the original DNSR plan); improving the Andover & Redbridge Railway by widening and straightening (including doubling the tracks); building eastward and westward junctions near Southampton West Station; and a line to a new pier, parallel to and west of the Royal Pier.

Naturally, the LSWR and DNSR schemes were opposed by each other before a Parliamentary committee in April 1882, with the LSWR also receiving opposition (as previously mentioned) from the Southampton Corporation, Harbour Board and Chamber of Commerce, while resistance to the DNSR came from the Southampton Dock Company. In putting forward their case, the LSWR went to great lengths to point out that their proposals would be far cheaper to put into practice, compared with those of the DNSR which would require negotiating difficult gradients, and even then would not serve any particular place on the route which was not already reached by rail. In fact, with a junction between the two companies at Whitchurch, the LSWR felt that the DNSR could still reach Southampton by way of the proposed Hurstbourne to Fullerton line, without the need and expense of constructing southwards from Whitchurch.

The Parliamentary committee listened to both sides and after several weeks of consideration, came down in favour of the DNSR scheme, after deleting various clauses. The line was finally authorised on August 10th 1882.

Although the LSWR had been defeated, they appealed to the House of Lords and, following this appeal, the LSWR were allowed to construct their Hurstbourne to Fullerton line as the impressively named Northern & Southern Junction Railway, also authorised on August 10th 1882, with later deviations authorised on August 20th 1883.

As soon as Parliamentary approval had been received, the LSWR wasted no time in getting work under way for their new line, and quickly appointed the contractor Joseph Firbank to construct the line at a cost of £162,700, and the LSWR engineer William Jacomb to supervise the work as well as the upgrading of the Andover to Redbridge line.

Constructing what seemed quite a short line from Hurstbourne to Fullerton was not an easy task, especially with heavy earthworks required between the main line near Hurstbourne and Longparish. Many of the navvies who constructed the line, set up camp in the Longparish area of Harewood Forest at a spot which became known as 'Ten Huts', the name deriving from tin huts. Unfortunately, as with nearly all heavy railway construction, several navvies were killed while carrying out their work. One such person was John Jones who, in May 1884 while assisting with excavation, crushed his foot under falling earth. He was taken to Andover Cottage Hospital where his leg was amputated, but sadly he died the following morning.

As there had been a siding on the 'up' side of the main line at Hurstbourne since August 1871, to serve the Earl of Portsmouth's grain store (the Earl then living close-by at Hurstbourne Park), it was not so surprising that when the new line was authorised in 1882, the LSWR decided to open a station at this site.

In April 1885, the LSWR Secretary Mr. F.J.Macaulay wrote to the Board of Trade informing them as follows:-

> *L.S.W.R.*
> *Secretary's Office*
> *Waterloo*
> *April 23rd 1885*
>
> *Sir,*
> *I am desired to give you notice that this Company's new railway from Hurstbourne to Fullerton will be completed and ready for inspection in one month from this date.*
>
> *I am, Sir*
> *Your obedient servant*
>
> *F.J.Macaulay*

The line was duly inspected on May 22nd 1885 by Major Francis Marindin on behalf of the Board of Trade, and he stated that the line was in good order and was fit to open for passengers on June 1st 1885, but pointed out that the position of the signal at the junction with the main line at Hurstbourne required some attention, as he felt it was difficult to see on reaching the main line from the new line, which came in on a curve.

Major Marindin also reported that the initial service would start from the main line at Whitchurch until the planned link with the DNSR was carried out. The aim at this time was of course for a through route with the Midlands and the North of England. Major Marindin went on to state that, as all the stations between Whitchurch and Fullerton were not provided with engine turntables, all trains must stop at all the stations, and that footbridges might be required at both Whitchurch and Fullerton.

The LSWR took note of these suggestions and the line opened for passengers on June 1st 1885. The following day, the LSWR Chairman Mr. Ralph Dutton, and Secretary Mr. F.J.Macaulay confirmed in a joint letter to the Board of Trade as follows:-

> *L.S.W.R.*
> *Waterloo*
>
> *The London & South Western Railway Company undertake to stop all Trains at the Stations between Whitchurch and Fullerton as long as these Stations remain unprovided with Engine Turntables; and that, if the Board of Trade require, Footbridges shall be provided at Fullerton and Whitchurch in the event of the traffic continuing to run backwards and forwards between these stations for a longer period than one year from this date.*
>
> *Sealed and signed this second day of June 1885.*
>
> *Ralph Dutton. Chairman*
> *F.J.Macaulay. Secretary*

The *Andover Advertiser* reported the opening of the new line in their issue of Friday June 5th 1885 as follows:-

THE NEW RAILWAY

On Monday the branch line of the London & South Western Railway from Hurstbourne to Fullerton was opened for passenger traffic. This line connects the Basingstoke to Salisbury line at Hurstbourne, and the Andover, Redbridge and Southampton line at Fullerton; and apart from having stations at Wherwell and Longparish, is intended to expedite the journey between London and Bournemouth.

At present there are four trains on the line, which run in connection with the 6.35 a.m.; 9.00 a.m.; 11.45 a.m.; and 3.50 p.m. trains from Waterloo; the 7.50 a.m.; 10.40 a.m.; 1.45 p.m.; and 3.53 p.m. trains from Salisbury to Southampton; and leave the latter place at 7.50 a.m.; 12.45 p.m.; 3 p.m. and 5.32 p.m. for Waterloo. There is no Sunday trains on the new line.

Although the line was often referred to as a branch line, it was built as a double track line throughout and with the proposed link with the DNSR at Whitchurch on the main line, it was hoped that through traffic would soon develop.

As the line mainly followed the valley of the River Test, it became popular with anglers who came down to fish in the fine trout waters, and the railway became affectionately known as 'The Nile' and even 'The Nile Valley Railway', no doubt the River Test creating the same image to the late Victorians and Edwardians as the biblical River Nile.

One person who is said to have been very fond of the new line was Queen Victoria, who sometimes used the route on her way to the Isle of Wight, because of the fine views of Harewood Forest and the River Test.

The goods yard to the south of Wherwell Station soon after the line had opened.   Lens of Sutton

The approach road and station building at Wherwell during the LSWR period.   Lens of Sutton

The proposed link with the DNSR near Whitchurch never happened (even though some work on the connection did in fact take place, but was soon abandoned) and the line was really only of use as an alternative for the Basingstoke to Southampton main line, although in 1906 the LSWR were authorised to build a 21 chain curve from the Andover to Redbridge line just north of Redbridge, to join the Bournemouth line, seven chains west of the viaduct over the River Test. This development would have given the Hurstbourne-Fullerton line new hope with the possiblity of fast trains running from Waterloo to Bournemouth and Weymouth, which would avoid the congestion in the Eastleigh-Southampton area. Unfortunately, by 1909 nothing had been done and the LSWR even tried to have the plans for the original curve altered to 45 chains, but were refused. By June 1917 the LSWR decided to let powers for the original curve lapse.

During the early part of 1913, apart from the anglers who came to fish in the River Test, very few passengers made use of the rather grand stations at either Longparish or Wherwell and to economise, the LSWR advised the Board of Trade that they would be making the whole line between Hurstbourne and Fullerton into single track, and that the work would be completed and ready for inspection by July 19th 1913.

Major J.W.Pringle made an inspection for the Board of Trade on July 21st 1913, and approved the new method of working as a single line, on the condition that "an undertaking to work traffic upon the electric tablet method is furnished by the company". The signal boxes were removed at Longparish and Wherwell and were replaced by ground frames, and from then on, the line was worked by the electric Tyer's Tablet System No. 6 Instrument.

In 1914, James Taylor Limited set up a sawmill near Longparish Station and built a narrow gauge railway to link their works with the station yard.

H13 class Steam Railcar No. 9 at Longparish Station.   Lens of Sutton

During the 1914-18 war, the line was extensively used for troop movements, relieving the main line for other traffic. In 1915, Messrs. Kynock Limited of Birmingham erected a wood distillation factory ajoining Taylors Sawmill near Longparish Station and requested the LSWR to provide siding accommodation. The LSWR carried out this request and then asked the Board of Trade to inspect and sanction the work. Colonel E.Druitt inspected the new siding for the Board of Trade and approval was given on April 13th 1916. Over 100 people were employed at the Kynock factory, and a special daily train ran between Whitchurch and Longparish to convey many of them. The weekly output of products from the factory (ranging from charcoal to wood oil) was about 1000 tonnes, and nearly all of it was transported by rail. In 1917, the Government took over the plant, and worked it until July 1919 when production appears to have ceased.

Although passenger traffic was very light, both Longparish and Wherwell Stations continued to see a fair amount of goods service and by the early 1920's, as many as 30 wagons per day were put to use by Taylors Sawmill at Longparish, for receiving and dispatching timber products. Longparish also had two coal yards, and Kennedy and Kempe had set up an engineering works and were sending out heavy chains by rail, even as far away as Scotland. Wherwell was also kept busy by the nearby Chilbolton farmers who used the station as the main loading place for all their corn. They also dispatched pressed hay for the Army and baled straw for use on strawberry beds.

By 1923, the LSWR had become part of the newly formed Southern Railway at the time of the railway grouping and, with passenger traffic falling away, the line suddenly burst into life in April 1927 when Piccadilly Pictures filmed several scenes

Hay being loaded into wagons at Wherwell Station sidings in the early part of this century.

Lens of Sutton

for their cinema version of Arnold Ridley's play 'The Ghost Train', starring Guy Newall, Ilsa Bois, Louis Rolfe, Anna Jennings and John Maymore. (Longparish Station was mainly featured where scenes for the film were shot on April 11th, 12th and 13th but, other locations on the line were also used in this silent film). Some of the cast and crew were accommodated at the White Hart Hotel in Bridge Street, Andover. When the filming was over and the film company had left, the railway returned to it's sleepy rustic slumber which had set in before hand.

On December 15th 1929, the junction at Hurstbourne was altered and it came as no great surprise when the sparse passenger service was withdrawn completely on July 6th 1931, saving the Southern Railway a reported £1,389 per annum. The goods service continued to both Longparish and Wherwell Stations, as the Southern Railway felt that it would be too costly to arrange an alternative road service.

It is highly likely that some through passenger trains did in fact use the route after the passenger service had been withdrawn, but on May 29th 1934 the section of line between Hurstbourne Junction and a point just north of what is now the A303 road at Longparish was taken out of use and lifted. The last through train to run over this section and out on to the main line was a goods train containing all the stock from a farm at nearby Bransbury (owned by a Mr. Hamilton) consisting of cattle, carts, horses and even the employees.

From this time onwards the line really did become a branch, although it was in fact worked as a goods siding only from Fullerton, which by now had even lost the title of Junction.

One very unfortunate fatal incident occurred at Longparish Station in 1936 when Harry Kimber, a temporary office lad, accidently rode his cycle over the edge of the platform and hit his head on the track.

During World War II, the line surprisingly reached its peak when it handled a tremendous amount of military traffic, mainly at an RAF Maintenance Unit which was set up at Longparish as an ammunition storage depot in October 1942.

After nationalization in 1948, the Southern Railway became British Railways Southern Region and the new owners soon suggested closing the line, but were persuaded against it by the military authorities, who felt that the line still had a role to play in clearing up the area of the ammunition storage. In fact, it was not until the early 1950's that this work was considered to have been completed.

The final goods service over the line was on May 28th 1956. After this date, the line was used for the storage of condemned wagons and vans, and also testing the Southern Region's new diesel multiple units before they went into service in the area.

T9 class 4-4-0 No. 30730 waits at the branch platform at Fullerton in the early 1950's. Lens of Sutton

Description of the Route

Whitchurch - Hurstbourne - Fullerton *(When first opened)*
As previously mentioned, the original service ran from Whitchurch to Fullerton with of course, the hope that a connection with the DNSR at Whitchurch would eventually be built. With this in mind, the LSWR added a platform at Whitchurch Station behind the main 'up' platform to accommodate the traffic for the new line.

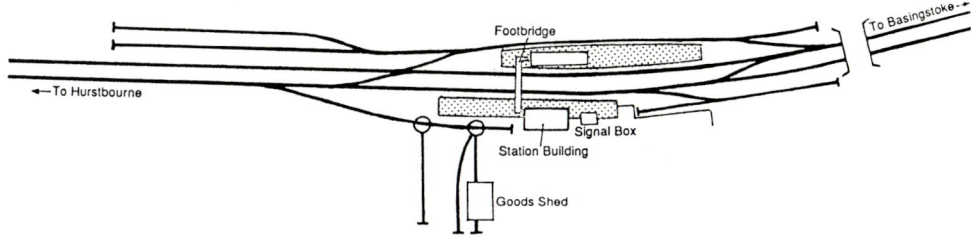

WHITCHURCH

Whitchurch Station in 1906, looking west towards Hurstbourne. The platform for traffic from Fullerton is on the right, while the branch train is berthed in the siding on the left. P. Trodd Collection

From Whitchurch, trains for Fullerton would cross over to the main 'down' line and then head west, first climbing a 1 in 1320 gradient, and then dropping a 1 in 194 to Hurstbourne, which was 2 miles from Whitchurch. A siding had been in existence on the 'up' side of the main line at Hurstbourne since August 1871, to serve the Earl of Portsmouth's grain store, so when the new line to Fullerton was approved, the LSWR wasted no time in building a station by adding wooden platforms on both the 'up' and 'down' sides of the main line. Each platform was provided with a wooden shelter while the 'up' platform also had a toilet. In fact, when the station was inspected by Colonel Yolland R.E. for the Board of Trade, he mentioned that he was reasonably satisfied with the work carried out but was concerned that no toilet was provided on the 'down' platform. When told that few trains would stop at Hurstbourne, Colonel Yolland then agreed that the station could open.

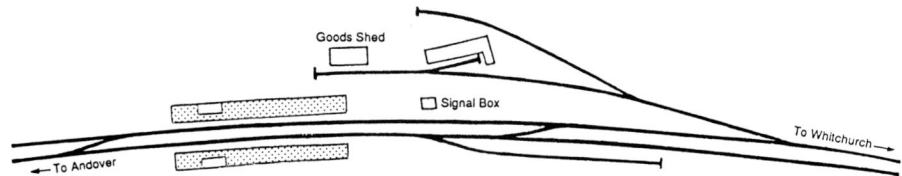

HURSTBOURNE

Hurstbourne Station on the main line, looking towards Whitchurch, soon after the station was opened. *Lens of Sutton*

From Hurstbourne, the Fullerton trains continued on the main 'down' line, crossing over the viaduct and after about ½ mile, the double track route to Fullerton curved away to the left and headed south in the direction of Longparish. Between the main line and Longparish, the line passed under and over several bridges, while first climbing a 1 in 500 and a 1 in 105 gradient, then dropping at 1 in 105,1 in 300, 1 in 105 (again) and 1 in 120, before reaching Longparish Station which was on the level. This section mainly ran through cuttings, which at times were as deep as 50 ft. in places and quite often needed the carriage lights on.

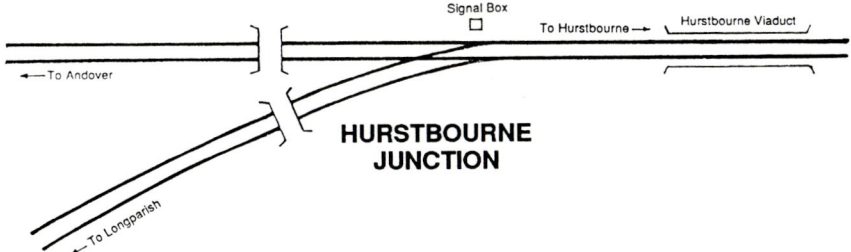

HURSTBOURNE JUNCTION

The station at Longparish was originally spelt Long-Parish but changed to one word in 1890. It was situated on the south side of the A303 road, 1½ miles from the very attractive village of Longparish, which is on the north side of the A303 and, as the village name suggests, extends for nearly 2 miles along the Test Valley. The station was 4¼ miles from Hurstbourne and gave the appearance of a rather grand country station with two platforms, both complete with large curved shelters. Sidings were situated behind the 'up' platform. The impressive station buildings were completed in 1884 and proudly displayed this date above the main entrance. A signal box with 15 levers was on the 'down' side of the approach to the station from Hurstbourne.

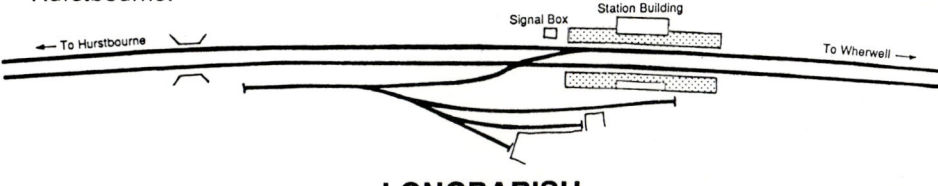

LONGPARISH

Early days at Longparish Station, looking north towards Hurstbourne.   N.J.Lambourne Collection

From Longparish, the line continued for just over 2 miles, first on the level and then dropping at 1 in 105 before reaching Wherwell Station, which was on the level and was approached through a deep cutting and passing under two bridges. Wherwell Station was situated very close to the lovely village of Wherwell, where black and white thatched roofed cottages are clustered at the foot of a steep hill. The station in many ways resembled Longparish, with similar station buildings giving the date 1884 over the main entrance, and large curved shelters on both platforms as well. The 15 lever signal box was at the southern end of the 'down' platform, while several sidings were situated on the south side of the 'up' line.

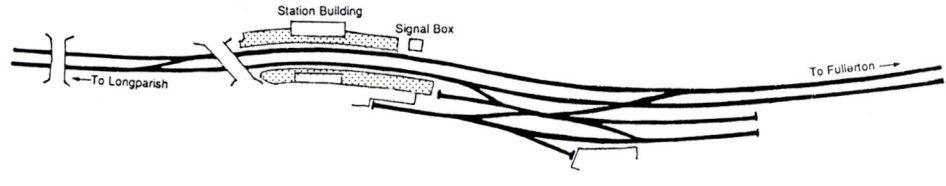

WHERWELL

Looking towards the approach to Wherwell Station from Longparish, soon after the line was opened. *P.Trodd Collection*

Early days at Wherwell Station, looking north towards Longparish.　　　Lens of Sutton

This view was taken during the same period, looking south towards Fullerton.　　　Lens of Sutton

From Wherwell, the line continued for about 1¼ miles on the level and then dropped at 1 in 115 and then 1 in 306, before reaching Fullerton Junction on the level. The original station at Fullerton was opened as Fullerton Bridge, when the Andover to Redbridge line was opened in 1865, and was situated near the road between the River Test and the River Anton. In 1871 the station was re-sited nearer to the River Test and when the line to Hurstbourne was opened in 1885, received the rather grand title of Fullerton Junction. The layout here for the new line consisted of double tracks and, like all the other stations on the line, included platforms with shelters, taking the overall platform total (including the Andover to Redbridge line) to four. Not bad for a very sparsely populated area.

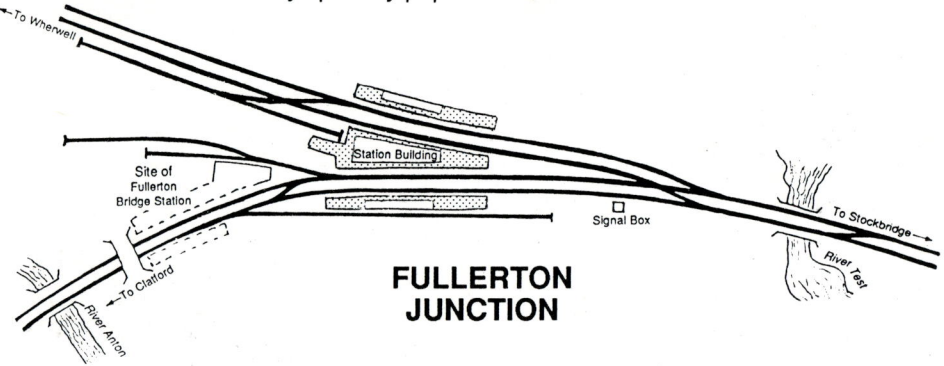

FULLERTON JUNCTION

A12 'Jubilee' class 0-4-2 No. 614 waits at Fullerton Junction with a single carriage for Whitchurch.
Lens of Sutton

Fullerton to Longparish *(After the passenger service had been withdrawn)*
With the whole length of the original double track line reduced to single track in July 1913, and the passenger service withdrawn in July 1931, the line was cut back in May 1934 to just north of Longparish Station, on the north side of the main A303 road, making this once through railway line into a branch line.

With the passenger service withdrawn in July 1931, the station at Fullerton had already lost its title of Junction in July 1929 (no doubt in anticipation), even though the line to Longparish stayed open for goods until May 1956.

Looking north at Fullerton Station with the branch to Longparish on the right. The late H.C.Casserley

Wherwell Station looking towards Longparish in 1951. R.M.Casserley Collection

A new siding at the north end of Fullerton Station was brought into use in October 1942 between the main Andover to Redbridge line, and the branch, which necessitated the cutting back of the length of the 'up' branch platform.

Wherwell Station was reduced to just one siding after the line was singled, but apart from this remained unchanged.

At Longparish, extensive work was carried out and sidings were added to serve the military traffic which the RAF Maintenance Unit had set up in October 1942 as an ammunition storage depot.

Looking north at Longparish Station showing the large concrete area where ammunition was loaded and unloaded during World War II. Lens of Sutton

The end of the line, just north of Longparish Station. October 9th 1957. S.C.Nash

Motive Power and Rolling Stock

When the idea for the line was originally conceived, the hopes were that it would be used as a link between the south coast, the midlands and the north, and that all sorts of through traffic would be seen. Unfortunately, the grand ideas were doomed before the line got started and the lightly used shuttle service between Whitchurch and Fullerton was mainly handled by some of the smaller LSWR locomotives, designed by either William Adams, the LSWR locomotive superintendent from 1878 to 1895, or his successor from 1895 to 1912, Dugald Drummond. These locomotives ranged from Adams O2 class 0-4-4T's to Drummonds C14 class 2-2-0T's.

In June 1906, the Andover Shed took delivery of LSWR H13 class Steam Railcars No. 11 and 12 (designed by Drummond), for use between Whitchurch and Fullerton. These Railcars were introduced by the LSWR as an economy measure for certain branch lines and short distance passenger services, and the two which were received at Andover proved to be quite popular at first, one journey per day being extended from Whitchurch to Basingstoke. Railcar No. 9 also saw service on the line. Unfortunately, the popularity and novelty of the Steam Railcars on this line did not last that long and they were withdrawn in February 1910.

The sparsely used passenger service returned to conventional working with a locomotive, and two or sometimes a single carriage, but in March 1928 a four-wheeled Drewry Petrol Railcar was also tried on the line. Built in 1927, this vehicle was yet another attempt at rural line economy but was unsuccessful and in 1930 it went to Ashford in Kent where it was rebuilt and worked for a time on the New Romney branch, until it was later sold to the Weston, Clevedon & Portishead Light Railway in 1934.

The last few years of passenger service between Whitchurch and Fullerton was mainly handled by Adams A12 'Jubilee' class 0-4-2's and what became the familar sight of a single carriage.

After the passenger service was withdrawn, the goods service from Fullerton to Longparish was worked by either Drummonds 700 class 0-6-0's, or his T9 class 4-4-0's, and occasionally in later years by a Bulleid Q1 class 0-6-0.

C14 class 2-2-0T No. 742 with the Fullerton train at Whitchurch Station in 1906. Lens of Sutton

H13 class Steam Railcar No. 12 at Hurstbourne Station en route for Fullerton. Lens of Sutton

A12 'Jubilee' class 0-4-2 No. 614 at Longparish Station. Lens of Sutton

The Drewry Petrol Railcar which was used on the line in the late 1920's. Seen here in March 1933 at New Romney in Kent.
The late Dr. I.C.Allen

Single carriage with A12 'Jubilee' class 0-4-2 No. 614 at Wherwell Station.
P.Trodd Collection

'0460' class 4-4-0 No. 0478 with single carriage at Wherwell Station on April 30th 1928
The late H.C.Casserley

T9 class 4-4-0 No. 30707 pulls a special inspection train under the Wherwell road bridge, as it heads towards Longparish from Fullerton on October 30th 1957, seventeen months after the line was officially closed.
S.C.Nash

Operation

When the line was originally built, signal boxes were required at both intermediate stations as well as the junctions at both ends of the line. The boxes at Longparish and Wherwell contained 15 levers.

On July 17th 1913, when the whole length of the line was reduced to a single track, the signal boxes at Longparish and Wherwell were replaced by ground frames and the line was then worked by the Tyer's Tablet System No. 6 Instrument.

After the line was lifted between Hurstbourne Junction and Longparish on May 29th 1934, the line between Fullerton and Longparish was then worked as a siding, by introducing the 'One Engine in Steam' principal. Stations and sidings were released by a key on the train staff. The signal box at Hurstbourne Junction was closed on October 10th 1934.

Southern Railway Sectional Appendix. March 26th 1934.

BETWEEN LONGPARISH AND FULLERTON.

Working of goods trains.—In order to provide the requisite brake power for safely controlling a down goods train, the load of which is in excess of equal to 25 wagons, on the falling gradients between Longparish and Wherwell, and between Wherwell and Fullerton stations, the Guard of such train must ascertain from the Driver before leaving Longparish or Wherwell, as the case may be, what number of wagon brakes are required to be pinned down and arrange for the train to be brought to a stand before descending the gradient to Wherwell or Fullerton respectively, so that wagon brakes may be applied accordingly.

The undermentioned table may be regarded as indicating the minimum number of brakes that should be pinned down over the sections of the line indicated, but, in the discretion of the Driver, more brakes may be applied according to necessity arising from abnormal weather conditions, or other unfavourable circumstances.

Load equalling (exclusive of brake van .	No. of wagon brakes to be pinned down with 20-ton brake van behind. See Note A.	No. of wagon brakes to be pinned down with 10-ton brake van behind. See Note B.
50	10	13
45	8	11
40	6	9
35	4	7
30	2	5
25	Nil	3
20	Nil	1

Note A.—A 20-ton brake van to be provided, whenever possible, at the rear of all up and down goods trains between Longparish and Fullerton.

Note B.—To apply in the event of a 20-ton brake van not being available at any time.

The Driver must be informed by the Guard the number and class of vehicles forming the train, and the Guard will be responsible for releasing the brakes on arrival at Longparish, Wherwell or Fullerton.

Engines.—For general purposes the axle load of engines working between Longparish and Fullerton in each direction must not exceed 16 tons 7 cwt. on the driving axle.

Gradient Profile

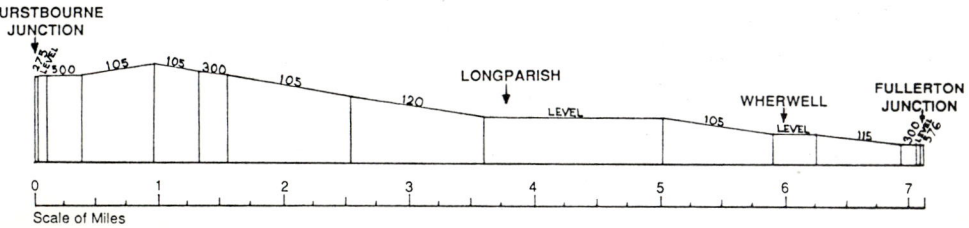

Timetables and Tickets

FEBRUARY 1890
BASINGSTOKE, WHITCHURCH, and FULLERTON.—L. & S. W.

Waterloo Station,	mrn	mrn	mrn	mrn	mrn	aft	aft	Docks Station,	mrn	mrn	mrn	aft	aft	aft
LONDON 48....dep	6 50	9 0	....	1115	1145	....	3 50	64 SOUTHAMPTON..dep	....	9 45	....	1245	3 5	....
Basingstoke......dep	8 27	1016	....	1245	1 32	....	5 21	Fullerton Junc...dep	8 0	1045	1145	1 50	4 20	....
Oakley	8 37	....	....	1255	1 44	....	5 30	Wherwell............	8 4	1049	1149	1 54	4 32	....
Overton............	8 44	....	....	1 2	1 51	....	5 36	Long-Parish........	8 10	1056	1156	2 0	4 53	....
Whitchurch 1.....	8 58	1035	1115	1 10	1 59	2 40	5 55	Hurstbourne 48....	8 19	11 5	12 5	2 10	5 6	....
Hurstbourne	9 4	....	1120	1 15	....	2 45	6 0	Whitchurch 1	8 33	1131	1210	2 26	5 12	6 10
Long-Parish	9 12	....	1127	1 22	....	2 53	6 7	Overton.............	8 41	1140	1218	2 44	....	6 18
Wherwell	9 19	....	1132	1 28	....	2 59	6 13	Oakley	8 49	1148	1225	2 52	....	6 25
Fullerton Junc. 64 arr	9 22	....	1135	1 31	....	3 3	6 17	Basingstoke 49, 8 arr	8 56	1157	1233	3 2	....	6 33
64 SOUTHAMPTON DKS.. arr	1021	....	1232	....	....	4 50	7 24	LONDON 49....arr	10 5	17 2	10 4	43	....	7 55

JULY 1924
WHITCHURCH and FULLERTON.—Southern.

Miles		Week Days only.					Miles		Week Days only.				
		mrn	mrn	aft	aft				mrn	mrn	aft	aft	
	143 London (Waterloo) dep	6 30	3 30	5 0	....	....		Fullerton Junction....dep	7 39	9 10	6 10	....	....
	Whitchurch.......dep	9 5	5 13	6 50	....	....	1	Wherwell..............	7 33	10 14	6 13	....	....
1½	Hurstbourne	9 10	5 18	6 55	....	....	3½	Longparish	7 40	10 24	6 20	....	....
6	Longparish	9 21	5 27	7 4	....	....	7	Hurstbourne..........	7 52	10 31	6 31	....	....
8	Wherwell.....(174	9 26	5 32	7 9	....	....	9	Whitchurch** (143..arr	7 57	10 36	6 36	....	....
9½	Fullerton Junc. 170, arr	9 30	5 34	7 13	....	....	65	152 London (Waterloo) arr	9 57	12 19	8 29	....	....

a Through Train to Southampton Terminus, see page 172.   b Runs from Southampton Terminus, see page 174.
** About 1¼ miles to G. W. (late D. N. & S.) Station.

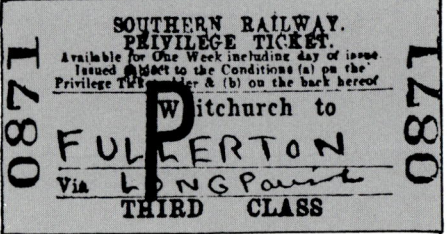

Tickets from the G.R.Croughton Collection.

Looking towards Wherwell Station from the deep cutting between the two overbridges.
October 30th 1957.

S.C.Nash

The Branch in World War II

The sleepy existence of the branch line to Longparish was shaken in 1942, when the RAF decided to set up a maintenance unit for ammunition storage in nearby Harewood Forest. The reason why the RAF chose this area could well be explained in the private personal memoirs of Mr. C.N.Anderson, who was assistant to the Southern Railway Divisional Superintendent at Southampton during World War II. Mr. Anderson writes as follows:-

"A telephone enquiry from Waterloo' *Can you suggest a stretch of woodland not too close to a town, rail served and about 25 miles inland?'* I suggested Harewood Forest between Andover and Micheldever. Within a week two RAF high-ups visited Harewood Forest and said at once it was the very place they had been looking for and, that was how the RAF Depot at Longparish came to be"

The RAF siding to the north of Longparish Station was brought into use on November 24th 1942, and other war time alterations included a new loop siding, built on the site of the 'up' side of the original double track, which was lifted in 1913.

The ammunition stored by the RAF in Harewood Forest was mainly bombs and bullets, which were kept in small huts, linked to the railway siding by concrete roads. The ammunition was unloaded from the trains with the help of mobile cranes and then driven to the huts by the RAF, using small tractors and trailers.

By the end of 1943, nearly 600 wagons of blockbuster bombs arrived by rail each month and by June 1944, it was rumoured that as many as 6000 wagon loads of bombs and bullets were stored in Harewood Forest.

After the war was over and troops returned home for demobilisation, the nearby Barton Stacey Camp was used to house the Americans and some reports state that in one evening alone, as many as 14 troop trains travelled up the line to Longparish.

At about the same time, the ammunition store in Harewood Forest was increased, when other similar units, which were being closed down elsewhere, sent their stocks to Harewood Forest for disposal. Some of the ammunition was sold and transported abroad, while the job of cleaning up and transporting for disposal took some years, and it was not until the early 1950's that the task was considered to be over.

Longparish Station while the area was used for ammunition storage in nearby Harewood Forest. Note the 'No Smoking' sign on the station platform.
Lens of Sutton

Final Closure

From the early 1950's, the line was down to just one goods train a day under the supervision of Lester Whitemore who, having been appointed stationmaster at Fullerton in 1940, was now in charge of five other stations in the area. Fifteen year old David Purkis joined the railway in January 1955 while living at Andover and had to cycle to Fullerton, then on to Wherwell and Longparish each working day, to deal with the paperwork of goods being delivered or dispatched, and assist with the shunting. He would then return to Fullerton before cycling back to Andover. The total daily distance was approximately 20 miles. Another task was to collect the weekly rent from the tenants of the station cottages at Longparish.

Fifteen year old David Purkis (left) with stationmaster Lester Whitemore at Longparish Station. July 9th 1955.

D. Purkis Collection

By March 1956, the service was down to one train (normally a T9 class 4-4-0 locomotive with a brake van carrying drinking water) on Mondays, Wednesdays and Fridays only. With such a sparse service, it was not surprising that British Railways Southern Region decided to close the line on May 28th 1956, with T9 class 4-4-0 locomotive No. 30288 pulling the last goods train from Longparish.

The driver of the last official goods train E. Chivers receives the key to the branch from stationmaster Lester Whitemore before leaving Fullerton for Longparish. May 28th 1956.
The late C.E.Wardell. Courtesy of D.W.Lindsell

The last goods train poses for this photograph at Wherwell Station en route to Longparish on May 28th 1956.
The late C.E.Wardell. Courtesy of D.W.Lindsell

Driver E. Chivers and fireman C. Matthews pose for this photograph at Wherwell Station. May 28th 1956.
The late C.E.Wardell. Courtesy of D.W.Lindsell

Stationmaster Lester Whitemore (left) shakes hands with 76 year old retired ganger Bill Taylor (of Longparish), as T9 class 4-4-0 No. 30288 prepares to leave Longparish at the official closing of the branch. May 28th 1956.
The late C.E.Wardell. Courtesy of D.W.Lindsell

The line was then used to store condemned vans and wagons before they were scrapped. Also, in 1957 the Southern Region's new diesel multiple units were tested on the line before they went into service in the area.

The branch was finally taken out of use on April 20th 1960, although a short section at Fullerton was left as a siding until June 1st 1964.

Passenger services between Andover and Southampton via Redbridge, were also withdrawn on September 7th 1964, and the line between Andover and Kimbridge Junction (north of Romsey) was closed completely, although the track remained in position for four more years.

Hurstbourne Station, on the main Basingstoke - Salisbury line, stayed open until April 1964, even though the section between Hurstbourne Junction and Longparish had been closed since May 1934.

Condemned electric stock, in the shape of '4 Sub' No. 4348, stored on the remainder of the branch at Fullerton in the early 1960's.
The late C.E.Wardell. Courtesy of D.W.Lindsell

Condemned wagons and vans at Longparish Station after the line had officially closed.
Lens of Sutton

The Present Scene

The site of Fullerton Station is very overgrown and appears to be just a footpath as you walk through the woods between the River Test and the River Anton, but a close inspection shows the outline of the former platforms, although many trees have grown on the trackbed of the Longparish line. In fact, it is now so overgrown that it has become impossible to walk the trackbed at this spot.

The first overbridge on the road to Wherwell is still in position, although there is no evidence of the former railway on either side. The embankments can still be spotted from the road as you approach the village of Wherwell, where the original station building is now a private residence, whilst new bungalows have been built nearby on the former trackbed.

The bridge which carries the road from Fullerton to Wherwell over the former branch. February 27th 1992. *Author*

The former station building at Wherwell. October 30th 1991. *Author*

The girder bridge, which carries the main road from Wherwell to Andover, is still in use and crosses over the former railway as does the next bridge, and from where the deep railway cutting can still be seen. Between here and Longparish, the high embankments can be seen from the road.

At Longparish, the former station building is (like Wherwell) a private residence, while the bridge which carried the line over the A303 road, was demolished in 1961 by the Royal Engineers.

Between here and the main line at Hurstbourne Junction, parts of the very deep former railway cuttings can still be seen in many places, while the site of Hurstbourne Station is now occupied by a scrap metal dealer.

At Whitchurch, the platform used by trains from Fullerton is still visible, although the track was downgraded to a siding in August 1939, and finally taken out of use and lifted in December 1966.

The road bridge which crosses over the former railway between Longparish and Hurstbourne Junction near Middleton Farm. February 27th 1992. Author

The skew bridge near Apsley Farm looking towards Hurstbourne Junction. This bridge was built with twin brick arches for the double track. February 27th 1992. Author

Conclusion

When the original Hurstbourne to Fullerton line was opened, the driving force to the LSWR was, of course, the plans at Whitchurch for a connection with the DNSR. Apart from offering an alternative to Southampton, the LSWR felt that this new route would also protect their territory in the Bournemouth and Weymouth area. After plans for the connection at Whitchurch were dropped, the LSWR turned their attention towards the curve just north of Redbridge, which would offer an even quicker route from London to Bournemouth, but even though they were authorised to build this curve, they surprisingly let their powers drop.

From then onwards, the future for the Hurstbourne and Fullerton railway was well and truly doomed, and the line became a forgotten byway, which really only saw any great activity during World War II.

Acknowledgments

Many thanks to the following people and organisations for their kind help in compiling information and supplying photographs for this publication:
Mr.P.Trodd, Mr.G.Jacobs, Mr.D.W.Lindsell, Mr.J.Burrell, Mr.B.Hilton, Mr.S.C.Nash, Mr.G.R.Croughton, Mr.R.M.Casserley, Mr.J.L.Smith of Lens of Sutton, Mr.A.A.Jackson, Mr.D.G.Purkis, Mr.N.J.Lambourne, Mr.E.J.Smith, Mr.G.Howell, Mr.J.Rose, the Andover Advertiser, the Public Records Office at Kew.
Thanks also to my son Paul for reading my text and to Mr.J.O.Christian of Binfield Printers Limited for his help.

Bibliography

THE LSWR Volume 2 by R.A.Williams
LSWR LOCOMOTIVES: THE ADAMS CLASSES by D.L.Bradley
LSWR LOCOMOTIVES: THE DRUMMOND CLASSES by D.L.Bradley
THE HISTORY OF THE HURSTBOURNE AND FULLERTON RAILWAY by Ed Goodridge
ANDOVER TO SOUTHAMPTON by Vic Mitchell and Keith Smith
RAILWAY MAGAZINE (Various issues)

The first bridge (centre of photograph) which crosses the former route to Fullerton at the remains of Hurstbourne Junction. The main Basingstoke - Salisbury line is in the foreground. February 27th 1992.   Author